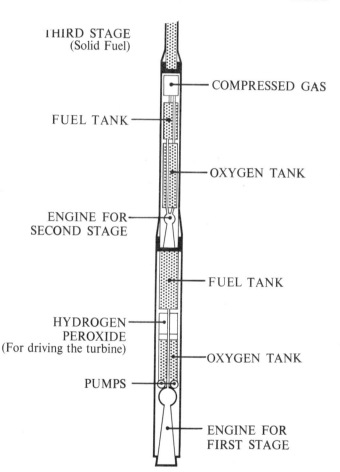

ARTIFICIAL
EARTH SATELLITE

THIRD STAGE
(Solid Fuel)

COMPRESSED GAS

FUEL TANK

OXYGEN TANK

ENGINE FOR
SECOND STAGE

FUEL TANK

HYDROGEN
PEROXIDE
(For driving the turbine)

OXYGEN TANK

PUMPS

ENGINE FOR
FIRST STAGE

THREE STAGE ROCKET
FOR SATELLITE LAUNCHING

Series 601

*This book tells the story of man's achieve-
ments in space, and of the tremendous
progress being made towards learning more
of the Universe in which we live, and towards
the day when man can travel to the moon—
and beyond!*

*Each page of the interesting text is accom-
panied by a superb full-colour illustration.*

A LADYBIRD
ACHIEVEMENTS
BOOK

2⁄6
NET

A LADYBIRD 'ACHIEVEMENTS' BOOK

EXPLORING SPACE

by
ROY WORVILL, M.Sc.

with illustrations by
B. KNIGHT

Publishers: Wills & Hepworth Ltd., Loughborough
First published 1964 © *Printed in England*

Storybook Space-flight

Although we think of rockets and space-travel as very new, men have dreamed for centuries about flying. They longed to soar and glide with the ease and grace of the seagull and the swallow.

A Greek writer nearly two thousand years ago wrote about a ship which was caught in a water-spout and carried up to the moon. Later he described how another daring explorer made a pair of wings and set out upon a voyage to the moon from the top of Mount Olympus, the home of the old Greek gods.

For a long time after this we do not find much about journeys into space. Then the telescope was invented and men began to learn more about the sky. A famous astronomer, named Kepler, discovered the laws which control the movements of the planets and he wrote a book telling about a voyage to the moon. Kepler's hero travelled there by the simplest way of all, by magic! He knew that there was no air between the earth and the moon and could think of no other way of getting there.

In 1638 a bishop, named Francis Godwin, told of a traveller who was carried to the moon by ten wild swans, a strange flight which you can see in the picture opposite.

A French author, Jules Verne, who lived a hundred years ago, wrote a book entitled 'From the Earth to the Moon.' His voyager was fired from a great gun, but Jules Verne forgot two very important things. His traveller would have been killed by the explosion, or roasted by the heat produced as the great shell rushed through the air.

The flight of the wild swans

7214 0139 2

Fireworks and Weapons

The first rockets, fired by gun powder, were made over seven hundred years ago by the Chinese. They were simply fireworks, just like the Guy Fawkes rockets which light up our skies every year on November 5th.

Rockets were later used for carrying life-lines to rescue sailors from wrecks or from the water. Some people thought rockets might be used in place of guns in time of war, but it was found that guns were far more accurate than any rocket which could then be made.

After the war of 1914-18 a new interest was taken in development of rockets. The chief reason for this was that men had now learned how to fly. But space-flight is very different from flying an aeroplane.

An aircraft must have oxygen to burn its fuel and provide power to drive it. Air must flow over and under its wings to support it. How could anything hope to fly without air?

The foundations of rocket-flight were laid by a Roumanian scientist and mathematician, Hermann Oberth.

Other experiments were made in America and Germany at this time. A leading German rocket-scientist, Wernher Von Braun, led experimental work in Europe. He now helps America's plans for exploring space, but during the last war it was his skill which enabled Germany to build her powerful rocket weapon known as the V2. It caused terrible loss of life and destruction to our cities, especially London.

Launching a rocket—on November 5th

Driving the Rocket

If you have ever fallen off a bicycle, or bumped your head, or simply walked a single step, you have experienced one of the most important laws about the way things move. It was announced by the great scientist, Sir Isaac Newton, three centuries ago and says that action and reaction are equal and opposite. If we push against something, it will push back. The wheels of a car push against the road. The propeller of a ship presses against the water. When we walk, our feet press against the floor or the pavement. When we fire a rifle it is not only the bullet which is pushed. The rifle kicks back against our shoulder.

When we travel out beyond the earth's atmosphere into space, there is nothing to push against, and all the time the earth's gravity, acting like a great magnet, tries to pull us back. How can we drive our rocket through empty space?

The answer is really quite a simple one. Two things are needed. A supply of fuel is the first. But the fuel will not burn without air, and there is no air in outer space, so we must carry a supply of air in the rocket.

There are several kinds of fuel which can be used. One is alcohol, with liquid oxygen to provide the air to burn it. Another is hydrogen peroxide, which contains oxygen and also water. There is another important thing about the rocket. It will travel more swiftly in space than through air, for there is less resistance. The rocket speeds through space on its own gases.

Escaping from the Earth

The greatest high jumper in the world can lift himself no more than a few feet above the earth. With a balloon or a high-flying jet aircraft he can reach a height of several miles. Only the rocket will enable us to reach the vast emptiness of space.

The pull of gravity depends upon size, or, more accurately, upon what is called mass. This is the amount of material in an object. The closer an object is to a large body like the earth, the greater is the earth's pull. If we get away from it, the strength of the pull weakens. The high jumper quickly falls back to earth. To get right away he would have to leap into space at a speed of seven miles per second. This is called the earth's escape velocity.

To launch a rocket into space at this speed demands enormous power, and material strong enough to withstand the tremendous strains and the heat produced by friction as the rocket rushes through the air.

There is an easier way of launching our rocket. We start with a rocket which need not escape completely from the earth. On top of it we place another smaller one and even a third. These can be fired in turn as the first one reaches the end of its flight and falls to earth. As the rocket gets farther into space, the earth's atmosphere is left behind, and there is less resistance. The earth's gravity, too, grows weaker and in this way a high speed can be built up. At twenty-five thousand miles per hour our rocket will escape from the earth's pull and travel wherever it is steered.

10

Out into Space

As the moment for launching the rocket approaches, we can imagine the excitement in the minds of those who are watching. This is the climax of months of preparation. The count-down goes backwards, and when the count reaches zero there is a burst of flame and a roar of motors. The glow of the burning gases beneath the rocket can be seen many miles away.

The rocket moves slowly at first as it tears itself away from the launching pad. Then its speed increases and in a few moments it is no more than a white, fiery speck in the blue heavens. It is on its way towards the stars.

The miles we use to measure distance across the earth become very small when we get into space. The earth is twenty-five thousand miles round the equator. At nearly ten times this distance is our nearest neighbour in space, the moon, two hundred and thirty-eight thousand miles away. Of all the planets, Venus is the nearest; but even Venus comes no nearer to us than twenty-six million miles. The red planet Mars at its nearest is thirty-five million miles away, while the other planets are at vastly greater distances.

When we think of the stars it becomes very awkward to count in miles. The number is so vast that it has little meaning for us. We use the unit known as a light-year. Clearly our rocket has far to go.

The Earth from a space-craft

Round the Earth

A date which will go down in history books for a long time to come is October 4th, 1957. This was when the Russian scientists launched the first earth satellite. It has since been followed by many others, some carrying the first men into space.

As our earth and the other worlds belonging to the sun's family travel along their orbits, we may wonder what keeps them on their right course. One thing is the pull of the sun's gravity. If it acted alone this would pull all the planets into its vast furnace, where they would melt like snowflakes. The other force is one which comes from their movement. This tends to throw them out into space like a stone which is being swung round on the end of a string. These two forces just balance.

If a satellite is launched at a high speed, it may go far away from the earth and be lost. If the speed is not high enough it will fall back and be burned up as it rushes through the air. If we want the satellite to travel round the earth, it must be sent at the right speed, and this varies according to the distance of the orbit from the surface of the earth. If we want it to travel round at a height of two hundred miles it must have a speed of about eighteen thousand miles an hour. At this speed it can go on travelling round the earth for many years.

A satellite's orbit round the Earth

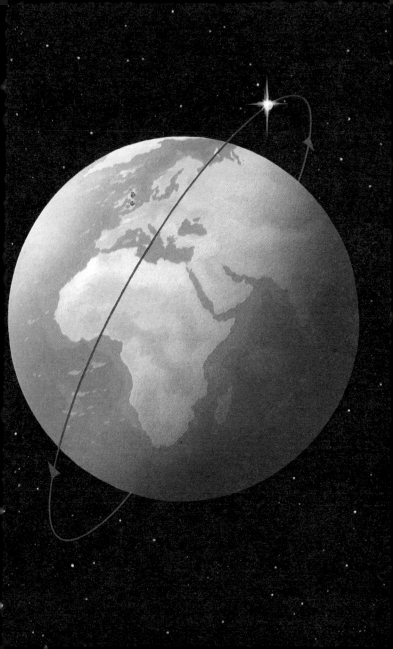

Space Rockets are Big

Scientists in America who are planning to explore space may build a rocket which will stand as high as a tall building, like St. Paul's Cathedral. Why is it necessary for rockets to be so large when it is much harder to lift a heavy weight than a lighter one?

The rocket which carried the American astronaut, Colonel John Glenn, into his orbit round the world, weighed 120 tons and was 80 feet high as it stood on the launching pad at Cape Kennedy (formerly Cape Canaveral). But the most important part of the rocket, the capsule, in which the astronaut travelled, held all the delicate instruments, radio, oxygen and safety equipment and weighed only a small fraction of the total—not more than one and a half tons. This part of the rocket is known as the payload. The rest of the weight was taken up almost entirely by fuel.

The fuel, and the material which supplied the oxygen to burn it, made up over one hundred tons of the total weight, while the rocket itself weighed no more than twelve tons.

The amount of fuel is heavy in itself; therefore it needs a lot of energy to lift it, which again means more fuel. Most of it is burned during the early stages of the flight when the earth's pull is strongest.

A lot of fuel needs large tanks to hold it, and, since empty tanks are only useless weight, some rockets have fuel tanks which fall away when empty.

A giant rocket shown beside the dome of
St. Paul's Cathedral

Steering the Space-ship

It would be useless to fit a space-ship with a rudder like that of a ship or aircraft. These rudders work because they have something to press against, as they are turned. The pressure on the face of the rudder gives a sideways push and changes the direction of the ship or aircraft.

How can we steer our space-ship when it is outside the air and there is nothing to press it against?

The rocket leaves behind a stream of hot gases from the burning fuel, and it is this stream of gas which drives the rocket. One way of steering the rocket is to fix a rudder or flat piece of metal, called a vane, at the back, where the gases will flow past it and push against it. In this way it will work like the rudder of a ship.

Another way is to build the rocket so that the combustion chamber, where the gases are burned, can be swung round to point in different directions. This changes the courses of the rocket by changing the direction of the push.

There is still another way in which this can be done. Several small combustion chambers in addition to the main one may be fitted. These can then be used to give a push in the required direction, either sideways or up or down, but we should remember that away from the earth those familiar words 'up' and 'down' have no real meaning. We must forget them entirely when we journey into space.

Altering course in space

No Brakes on a Rocket

With every kind of transport we use, making it move is only one part of the problem. The other, which is equally important, is to be able to slow down its movement and to stop it.

Land vehicles are fitted with brakes which usually work by causing friction on the wheels or other moving parts. We can stop a toboggan by applying the friction to the ground with our feet.

With no air or water, and no ground anywhere near it, the rocket cannot be slowed down by any kind of friction. Out in space, once it is moving, it will continue to move until something else either pushes against it or pulls it back. This is why it is important that the rocket is sent on its right course to begin with. A small error at the beginning could cause a very big one later on.

It is possible, however, to control the rocket after launching it into space, by using forward-pointing jets of gas like those which can be used to steer it. Far into space, where the pull of the earth's gravity is weakened, only a small push is needed to reduce speed, and one way of applying the push backwards, is by using containers of compressed gas which can be released a little at a time.

These backward-firing jets are sometimes called 'retro-rockets', and without them it would be impossible to slow down the rocket once it had been sent on its course.

Firing the retro-rockets to slow down the space-craft

The Astronaut in Flight

Let us see what happens as the rocket takes off with our astronaut securely strapped into his capsule in the nose of the great missile.

As you sit in a chair the seat supports you by pushing against you. The astronaut's seat not only supports him but lifts him up at very high speeds. It pushes against him far more strongly than our chair does against us. We say that he is under the strain of several gravities. If his seat was attached to a weighing machine it would show several times more than his normal weight.

When the rocket has reached a speed which will let the capsule travel on freely (in the correct orbit and without the need of motors), the rocket and capsule are separated. The astronaut is now in a strange state of weightlessness. If his space-craft was large enough, and he was not strapped down, he would float about like a thistle-down. To move about he would have to pull himself hand over hand along a wall, or kick against a wall, in which case he would move away in a straight line until he hit the opposite side.

Eating and drinking would bring some tricky problems. It would be impossible to pour a liquid down your throat. Your pen or pencil would float away from you if you let it go.

Inside the capsule

Return to Earth

There is no reason why a space-craft in orbit should not continue travelling round the earth for a very long time, since there is nothing to upset the balance of the forces which keep it in its place.

A man who is shut up inside such a small space, with only a limited amount of air, water and food, cannot stay alive for very long in those conditions. Apart from the strain on his body there is a very great strain on his mind. Space is very large and very lonely. Sooner or later he must be brought down to earth.

This is one of the most difficult problems which the space-scientists have had to solve. The hardest part is sometimes called the 're-entry problem'. It is not difficult to reduce the speed of the space-ship and allow the earth's pull to take effect. The important thing is to make sure that this happens gradually. If the earth pulls it back unhindered, the speed of its fall through the air will make it so hot that the craft will burn up like a shooting star.

First the space-craft must spiral slowly towards the earth by firing the retro-rockets to check the speed. As it enters the atmosphere a parachute is released and this enables the astronaut to make a safe landing, hoping that if all has gone according to plan there are ships and aircraft to transport him safely back home to tell of his great adventure in space.

Journey to the Moon

Some people think that it is a waste of time and money to send a manned space-craft to the moon. But this argument has been used about many other ventures, like the first aeroplane, or the voyage of Columbus. Men are always eager to find out more about the worlds around them, and we cannot be sure just which experiments are going to prove useful until we try them.

Until recently men thought of the moon as something very beautiful to look at but quite beyond reach. 'Crying for the moon' has always meant asking for something which can never be ours.

Now this idea is changing, for a space-craft sent from Russia has travelled round the moon and taken photographs of the far side which is always turned away from us, and other rockets have landed on the surface very close to the target areas.

Already we know a great deal about the moon from the use of telescopes and other instruments. It is a world of great extremes of temperature. When the sun is high in the sky the moon's surface becomes as hot as boiling water. At night it is frozen in intense cold. There is no air and it seems unlikely that any life exists on the moon.

But there are many questions to which we would like answers. What kind of soil and rock is there on the moon? Is there a layer of dust into which the space-craft may sink? What are the mysterious white rays which streak the face of the full moon like the lines on a peeled orange? Above all we want to know what made the many thousands of craters, great and small, which are scattered over the moon.

Preparing to land on the Moon

Stations in Space

An aircraft carrier is a ship which acts as a floating aerodrome. Space-craft, too, will need something like this in order to re-fuel and travel away on their long flights without coming back to earth. But there would be other uses for a space-station.

It could not stand still because the earth's gravity would pull it down. It would have to revolve around the earth just like the moon or an artificial satellite.

One suggestion is that it should be shaped like a wheel, about two hundred and fifty feet in diameter.

Another kind of platform in space was proposed by an Austrian engineer. It was to revolve much farther away from the earth, at over twenty thousand miles, where its speed would just match the speed of the earth's rotation. This would make it appear in a fixed position above one part of the earth like a star which always remains overhead.

There are very many difficult problems connected with the building of space-platforms of this kind, especially if they are designed to be occupied by human beings for periods of weeks or months. It seems very likely that the fully equipped space-station is something which lies in the distant future. The smaller unmanned satellite will probably serve many of our purposes for a long time to come.

A possible space-station in orbit

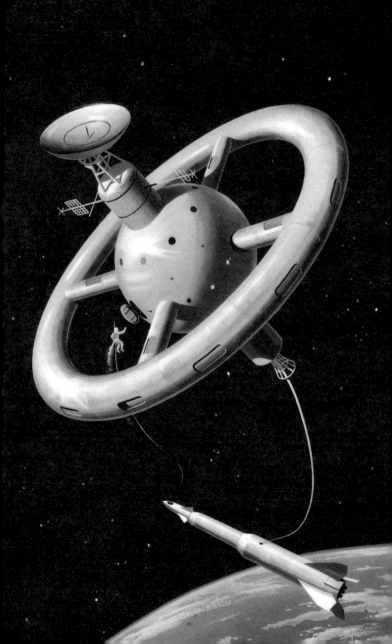

Target—the Moon

Let us suppose that we are aboard a rocket-ship bound for the moon. It is a journey which would take about three or four days, and as our rocket roars into the sky we watch the land and sea falling behind us. The clouds, too, are soon left behind and the sky becomes a darker blue. The curve of the earth is clearly visible from a hundred miles above its surface and, after a day's journey, our planet becomes a distant globe like a big full moon. It is a water-blue colour and streaked with patches of cloud, beneath which we can see areas of green and brown where the forests and desert lands are found. At the north and south poles are the white ice-caps.

The pull of the earth's gravity is weakening and the feebler pull of the moon is growing as we approach. There is a blaze of sunshine far more intense than we find on earth, but in the shadows, when the sun is not dazzling us, the brilliant stars shine out in a sky of velvet black.

We are falling at a speed of five thousand miles an hour towards a strange world of dusty plains, rugged mountains and great craters, which has remained almost unchanged for millions of years.

Our landing is controlled by a radar set in the rocket-ship which can judge our distance accurately. At the critical moment the forward-firing jets begin to blaze. We are feeling our own weight again as the engines reduce our speed. For a few seconds there is a cloud of fire and dust and then silence. We are on the moon.

Ready to leave the Moon

The Lunar Base

In some ways the moon is a better place for a space-station than one which is only a few hundred miles above the earth. There is no atmosphere to make the stars and planets twinkle; also the moon takes a month to turn on its axis instead of only a day. The stars would be visible for much longer and they could be seen even in the daytime. There would be no sunlight to dim their brilliance as happens in the bright blue skies we see above the earth.

Of course lunar explorers will have to eat and breathe. Oxygen must be provided to keep them alive. But not all the oxygen on the earth is found in our atmosphere. There is much in the rocks, too, although it is mixed with other things. It may exist in the rocks on the moon. Crops could be grown on the moon in specially sealed greenhouses, feeding on minerals dissolved in water. They would have fourteen days of continuous sunlight to help them grow.

Getting away from the moon would be much easier than getting away from the earth. Because of its smaller mass the moon's gravity pull is only a small fraction of that exerted by the earth.

How Much do We Weigh?

You have probably read about Sir Isaac Newton, and how he saw a falling apple and linked it up with the worlds in space through the law of gravity. This acts as though the earth were a great magnet which pulls things towards it. But we must think of the magnet as though it were not on the surface of the earth where we live, but buried deep at the centre, four thousand miles beneath our feet. Since the earth is not quite a sphere, but bulges round the equator and is slightly flattened at the poles, we are farther from the magnet at the equator than we are at the poles, and so we weigh a little less on the equator.

If we get four thousand miles from the earth's surface a pound weight would weigh only four ounces. A man who weighs twelve stones would weigh only three stones at the same distance. On the moon, where the gravity pull is only one sixth of that of the earth, our twelve stone man would weigh no more than two stones.

As we have already seen, the space-traveller who is going up in a rocket will weigh three or four times more than normal, the exact increase depending on the speed of the rocket and how quickly it is accelerating. The men who have circled the earth in a space-craft have first experienced this great increase in weight and then the complete opposite. Once in orbit they become weightless, because the speed of their space-craft as it circles the earth tends to throw them outwards, and this just cancels out the pull of the earth's gravity.

An astronaut floats without weight

The Planets Near the Sun

The nearest world to the sun is the little planet Mercury. It is not much bigger than our moon and very few people have seen it, although it shines quite brightly in the sky at certain times. In the British Isles and other northern countries it is best seen during the weeks of spring, when it comes for a few evenings into the western sky after sunset. It is always up there in the sky somewhere near the sun, but we can only see it when the sun is below the horizon and the planet is at its greatest distance from the dazzling sunshine. Mercury travels round the sun every eighty-eight days. It turns the same face towards the sun always, and for this reason it is intensely hot on that side. On the other side, strangely, where there is endless night, it is the coldest world of the solar system. Mercury would be a very unfriendly world for space-travellers.

Venus is a much larger planet, very much like the earth in size, but there are many mysteries about it. It shines very brightly in the night sky, or in the early morning sky before sunrise. It is covered with a thick layer of cloud. We can never see the surface of Venus and we do not even know how long it takes to turn round on its axis. Some space-probes have already been sent towards Venus and these will soon be followed by others. We have great hopes that one day we shall know what kind of a world this beautiful but mysterious planet really is.

36   *Little Mercury, the hottest and coldest world*

The Outer Planets

Beyond the orbit of our planet earth lies the red world of Mars. It is the only planet of which we can clearly see the solid surface. When it comes into our night skies, it shines with a bright orange-red light. Through a telescope we see the orange-red globe marked by patches and streaks of a blue-green colour. These dark patches may be some kind of plant life. The narrow streaks are the famous 'canals'. What they really are is one of the most fascinating things which the space-craft of the future may be able to tell us.

Outside the path of Mars are the two giant planets, Jupiter and Saturn. They are both very cold worlds and though very beautiful to look at, they are surrounded by dense atmospheres of poisonous gases. Although we cannot think of Jupiter with its twelve moons, and Saturn with its splendid rings, as likely homes for living creatures like ourselves, the space-craft equipped with instruments will doubtless one day tell us much more about them.

Far beyond Saturn are the other two giant worlds, Uranus and Neptune, about which we know very little as yet. They are so far from the sun that its feeble rays cannot give them much warmth, and they could not possibly support living things like those we know on earth.

At the outermost edge of the sun's kingdom is the little world called Pluto, much smaller even than the earth, and three thousand, six hundred million miles from the sun. Beyond Pluto there is only empty space and the stars.

The red planet, Mars, a world where life may exist

Out to the Stars

The sun is the nearest star. It seems so very much bigger and brighter than all the others only because it is so much closer. Other than the sun, the nearest star is to be found in a constellation called The Centaur. Unfortunately, if we live in the northern part of the world, we cannot see this constellation, as it lies in the southern hemisphere of the sky. The name of the star is Proxima Centauri.

Even Proxima Centauri is separated from us by many millions of millions of miles. The swiftest traveller we know is a ray of light. But light, speeding at one hundred and eighty-six thousand miles a second, takes over four years to reach us from this star. It would be a very long journey, even if our space-craft could travel at the speed of light.

Most of the stars we see in the heavens are far more distant. The brightest one in the whole sky is called Sirius, the Dog Star, and it is also nearer than most. Its light takes just over eight years to travel to the earth. Some other stars are so far away that the light rays must travel for many centuries across the vast space which separates them from us. No manned space-craft from earth is ever likely to travel so far or so fast. Oddly enough, however, it would take very little more energy to send a space-craft to a star than it would to one of the planets.

The space-craft in flight

Earth's Man-made Moons

Since the first man-made moon was launched in 1957 the number has steadily grown, and we are now beginning to realise that the artificial satellite is capable of doing much useful work.

If we want to send a radio message to a country on the other side of the world the problem is complicated by the earth's round shape. Radio waves, like light waves, travel in straight lines. To send radio waves round the world is like trying to see round a corner.

Sometimes, at a street corner, you may have seen a large mirror set up to show drivers and pedestrians if anything is coming from another direction. This is one way of seeing round a corner. Radio waves, too, will bounce off certain things and change their direction.

High up in the earth's atmosphere is a layer of air which will make some radio waves do this, and so a message can be sent round the world. This layer of air deflects the waves back to earth, and prevents them going straight out into space.

At certain times, however, this layer of air may be upset and fail to work properly. It frequently happens, for example, when there are many spots visible on the surface of the sun. A satellite which is high above the earth can be used to bounce radio waves back to another part of the world. Unlike the layer of air which does this, the satellite is not disturbed by sunspots and so it always works well. Television pictures are now sent over long distances by the same method.

A satellite, shaped like some strange creature from another world

Watching our Weather

From its lofty position a hundred miles or more above the earth, the satellite can keep a close watch upon the atmosphere and the cloud formations which cause our weather. The Tiros satellite was most helpful in tracking the fierce storms, known as typhoons, which could not be forecast by other means. One of these moons, Tiros III, found over fifty of the great storms and tracked them from their beginning to their end.

Satellites do not mean the end of weather stations on the ground, but they do give very great help to them.

Since the successes of the Tiros moons, others have been sent into space to help collect information of the same kind.

Satellites look at the earth and its atmosphere. They can look into space and find out much about the waves of radiation which never get to the earth because the atmosphere stops them. They can make measurements of the air, of temperature, of magnetism and of gravity around them. Unhappily, too, they could be used also for destructive purposes in time of war. We must hope that men will determine that the man-made moons shall be used only for peaceful purposes.

Satellites can warn us of storms like this

Dangers in Space

The layer of air around the earth protects us from many of the dangers which lurk in space. We depend upon the sun's rays for the light and warmth which keep us alive, but there are some kinds of rays from the sun which would burn us to death if we were not protected from them.

The sun gives out a great deal of ultra-violet light, for example. These rays travel in very short waves and our eyes cannot see them. Fortunately the air stops most of them from reaching us and a very thin layer of material, such as metal, or even some kinds of glass, could give complete protection.

From far out in space come other kinds of radiation known as cosmic rays. Some of these do get through the air to reach us, and out in space there must be far more of them. As yet we do not know very much about these rays or how great a danger they really are.

Every day our earth is bombarded by a rain of dust and pieces of stone and metal known as meteors. Most of these are burned up as they rush into the atmosphere. We see them flash across the night sky in the form of shooting stars although, of course, this name has nothing to do with the real stars. In space, however, where there is no atmosphere to shield the traveller, there must be a much greater chance of being hit by meteors and some of them may be quite large pieces of rock. At the high speeds of forty to sixty miles per second at which they move, they would certainly be able to do serious damage to a space-craft.

A rocket encounters a meteor swarm high in the earth's atmosphere

A Telescope in the Sky

Have you ever looked at something through the hot air above a burning fire or stove? If you have, or if you have looked across the countryside on a hot summer day, you will have seen that everything appears to be shimmering like the ripples on a pool of water.

When we look through a telescope this movement of the air is greatly magnified, and makes the view of a star or planet very unsteady. The twinkling of a star is caused by the same thing. It makes clear, sharp views of the moon, planets and stars impossible.

This is the reason why some astronomers and scientists are hoping that a fairly large telescope may be sent into space above the thick lower layers of the atmosphere. Already, telescopes have been sent up to a great height in balloons, and even in this way the photographs which have been taken with them have shown that the upper air is much clearer than the dense layers near the ground.

When a telescope can be sent into space, above the air, it will have a better chance of taking clear photographs of the sun, moon, planets and stars. Many scientists think that this would be a much better plan than taking all the trouble needed to send a man into space.

Taking pictures by telescope and camera
suspended from a high-altitude balloon

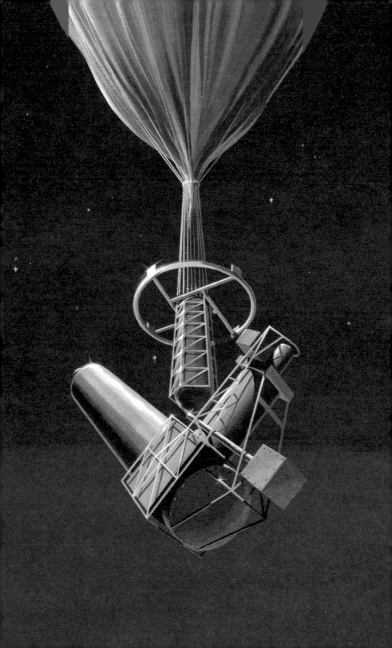

Life on Other Worlds

We have already seen that the planet Mars may possibly have some kind of plant life. Some people thought that intelligent beings lived there, too, and had built canals to carry water from the melting snows of the polar regions to the dry, desert parts of the planet.

Although this was a most interesting idea it is unlikely to be true. Regarding the possibility of life on the other planets, Mercury is too hot on one side and too cold on the other, and it has no atmosphere. We know little of Venus, but apart from Mars all the other planets seem certain to be far too cold for life. What can we say about other stars?

The stars themselves are very hot bodies like the sun and nothing could live on them. There may, however, be some which have planets like those which travel round our sun. An American astronomer has said that one of the nearer stars certainly has a large planet, bigger than Jupiter, revolving round it.

In our great Milky Way system, or galaxy, there are about one hundred thousand million suns. If we suppose that planets are very rare, belonging only to one in a million stars, it seems that there could still be many thousands of planets. Some of these might have life like that of our own world. It is also possible, of course, that in other parts of the universe there may be living things quite unlike us. One thing we do know is that the materials of which our world is made, the elements as they are called, seem to be much the same in every part of the universe.

SIGNPOSTS TO SPACE

There are no fixed distances in space, as everything is moving. The figures given below are approximate distances. For each planet, the figure given is when the earth and planet make their nearest approach to one another. However, a rocket travelling to a planet must follow a curved path which is much longer.

FROM THE EARTH TO

THE SUN - - - -	92,900,000 miles
THE MOON - - -	238,900 miles
MERCURY - - -	50,000,000 miles
VENUS - - - -	26,000,000 miles
MARS - - - -	35,000,000 miles
JUPITER - - -	390,000,000 miles
SATURN - - -	793,000,000 miles
URANUS - -	1,689,000,000 miles
NEPTUNE - -	2,700,000,000 miles

PLUTO — follows an unusual path round the sun. This can bring it inside the path of Neptune, as will happen from 1969 to 2009.

The nearest star is called Proxima Centauri, and its light takes just over four years to reach us, travelling at about 186,000 miles a second. A light-year, the unit we use to measure distances to the stars, is six million, million miles.